Visiting Hours

New York City Big Book Award Distinguished Favorite in Poetry, 2021
WINNER, Human Relations Book Award, 2021
WINNER, Best Book of Narrative Poetry, American Fiction Awards 2021
WINNER, Best Book of Religious Poetry, American Fiction Awards 2021
CIPA EVVY Best Book Award, Runner-Up, 2021
International Book Awards Book of the Year Finalist, 2021
Julie Suk Book of the Year Award Finalist, 2021
National Indie Excellence Book of the Year Finalist, 2021
Agha Shahid Ali Poetry Prize Finalist, 2018
Hudson Prize Finalist, 2018
Jake Adam York Poetry Prize Finalist, 2017
Georgia Poetry Prize Finalist, 2017
Miller Williams Prize Finalist, 2017
National Poetry Finalist, 2016
Akron Poetry Prize Finalist, 2015

VISITING HOURS

Andrew McFadyen-Ketchum

STEPHEN F. AUSTIN STATE UNIVERSITY PRESS
2020

Copyright © 2020 by Stephen F. Austin University Press

All rights reserved
Printed in United States of America

For information about permission to reproduce selections from this book, contact *permissions* :

Stephen F. Austin State University Press
P.O. Box 13007, SFA Station
Nacogdoches, TX 75962
sfapress@sfasu.edu
www.sfasu.edu/sfapress
936-468-1078

Project Manager: Kimberly Verhines
Typset in Garamond

ISBN: 978-1-62288-312-7

Second Printing

for Mary Interlandi
(1984-2003)

Marysarias

Forsythia in February ❧ 13
Smith Lake ❧ 14
Proffer Mountain ❧ 15
Visiting Hours ❧ 17
A Calling ❧ 26
On the 1ˢᵗ Anniversary of Mary's Death ❧ 28
Marysarias ❧ 29

Speak, Sad Child, Speak

Like the Dead ❧ 41
the catalpas they shudder the catalpas they step from their roots ❧ 42
Mare Orientale ❧ 43
Fast Freeze ❧ 44
Ice ❧ 45
when the spires of these high rises at last darken ❧ 54
Salvation ❧ 55
i shiver ❧ 56
I Too Grow Tired of Winter ❧ 57

A Star of the Sea

Night ❧ 65
Far from the Fields Turned Crystalline by Winter ❧ 70
Meditation on Balsam Mountain ❧ 75
The Lost ❧ 76
A Brief History of the Living World ❧ 78
On the 10ᵗʰ Anniversary of Mary's Death ❧ 84
On the 100ᵗʰ Anniversary of Mary's Death ❧ 87
Epistle ❧ 97

Acknowledgments ❧ 99
Notes ❧ 100
About the Author ❧ 101

*If you can think of the mind as a place continually
Visited, a whole city placed behind
The eyes, and shining, I can imagine, now, its end—*

—Larry Levis, "Winter Stars"

Forsythia in February

Rapid, their blooming overnight,
How they remind me another year has turned,

These boughs of yellow stars effulgent
At the feet of fence posts on the shoulders

Of empty highways, resplendent
These firebrands of a life half-remembered.

"My God," I say to these gold flames golden
Only briefly, "what's become of you, girl I loved?"

My God, I hear her say back, *boy who never said
I love you. What of these harsh winds?*

*What of this hard dream
Of yet another cold front*

Yet another dawn?

Smith Lake

We wanted to touch the moon, that flashbulb
   that bobbed on the heat-glazed pane of Smith Lake.
So we dove, Mary and I, fully-clothed from the dock,
   paddled slowly that body of water as chorus
Frogs and crickets boomed back and forth
   from the reed-thick shore. There, at the lake's
Dead center, we joined arms, our bodies
   ringing the moon's reflection. Treading water,
Mary cupped her palms beneath that beacon,
   lifted it to my lips, and said *Drink*.... And what
Could I do but follow when Mary side-stepped
   buoyancy and dove beneath the moon,
Dropped easily through zones of cold
   and colder water, the frog-slick star-vines
And hydrilla swaying heavily in the drifts, her hair
   held suspended by the water's hundred hands?
If only I could go back to the moon's conception
   when it first broke free of the earth to fly that first
Tethered orbit around the world. If only I could
   tell the Jade Rabbit's story, trace its outline
From ridgelines and craters like the Man in the Moon,
   that hare, lore says, grinding herbs in an urn
For the immortals, that moon returned
   to its rightful station overhead. I want you
To see Mary making small motions with her hands
   to keep from rising as we held our breaths who knows
How long until she rose, thick ribbons of reeds
   unraveling from her ankles, Mary surfacing
So slowly it was as if she climbed not water but sky,
   Mary backlit by darkness, Mary slipping
Into the moon.

Proffer Mountain

Even now, ten years later,
It's hard to believe
It was the road's grip alone
That kept us breathing.
No moonlight as we
Maneuvered the hairpins
And jogs of the fire road
We climbed. The New River
Hammering along in its groove
Through the chinquapins.
You could say we desired
Transcendence, wheeling
Our way up Proffer
Mountain, headlights
Panning wildly as broken
Lighthouse beams. You
Could argue we were just young,
Sleeping all day, flinting
Fires by night. No tent.
Only our mummy bags
And boots. The frayed edges
Of the tarp. Satellites pinging
Across the cool fix of stars.
It's Mary's voice, not these images
That keep calling me back.
That one evening of snow
That fell from the moon,
Its broad, almost winged flakes
Turning back into water
Just moments above
Our campfire's flames.
That weird metal ache of last dark.
Stoking the campfire all night
Until the faceplate

Of the ridgeline tilted open
And the sky's dull tint
Drained back into the valley
Like a bruise. It's Mary's face
Lit by fire. It's the nightjars
Calling out into the quiet
For a name: *Whip-poor-will?*
Whip-   or-will?
It's Mary saying back:
-will   -will   -will

Visiting Hours

       i

Then, we knew nothing of sadness. No suicide
Threats or institutional wards. Sleep came naturally
To us in our beds and when I dreamed, I dreamed
Of Mary. But on the phone, she was all stories

Of group therapy and the crazies who listed down
The long, pharmaceutical hallways. The fluorescents'
Strain when shock waves flagged the lines. How
When the twin red oaks bled their shadows

Past the gate, another night came calling. Still,
When the doctors' opinions turned and Mary
Came home, the ward's work became our own:
Antipsychotics and insomnia dreams,

The list of sharp objects we checked our world
Against. She shaved her head and called it liminal,
Slept by day and shook coffee to her mouth by night,
Sinking deeper and deeper into the diamond-blue oracle

Of her laptop when all but the clocks were sleeping.
When finally she did it, a year had passed
In that bedroom we swore not to enter: dim shafts
Of dust in beams through the blacked-out

Casements, the instructions Mary scrawled in black
Sharpie across her mirror:
                                                     WAKE

brush YOUR *teeth*
                    stop thinking SUCH THINGS

ii

No one prepared me my entrance
Into that ship of lost souls
Where Mary slept. No one
Taught me to mask each step I took
Across the checkered linoleum
Or that it wasn't "wandering,"
That path of pea gravel and weeds
That wound the back-lot's maze
Of fifty-year boxwoods and a crumbling
Slave wall, that path the doctors
Had Mary keep. Pulling handfuls
Of bluegrass and henbit, I brought
Her back to childhood's game of hands.
I turned her palm over in my palm,
Traced her birthline with the tip
Of a finger and read the will
Of the thumb, said, "you will name
Your many children for saints," only
To watch her turn her hand into a fist
Around another clump of thistle.
What could I do? I nothing
But a boy dangling before her,
Searching for the words
To summon the girl I once knew
From the girl she had become,
Her hair already turned the dun
Of the ash of her cigarette,
Her eyes turned all hours
To the closed doors of the earth,
Her down-turned lashes
The wings of some darkly-sane
And wing-broke bird.

iii

Her oversized t-shirt. Her paint-spattered
Jeans. Bras hung like fourth-notes

From the bed post. Prison bars of light
Then dark then light again cast by the south-

Facing window: None of it seemed real. I a member
Of the perfectly sane allotted his single hour.

So I took it all in: The displaced game pieces
And faded carpet, the gowned residents hugging

The ward's warped walls, the courtyard
Where I found her in a sanctum of smoke.

Standing in the doorway I held open,
I watched a rhombus of daylight scroll

Across Mary's star-turned face, her eyes
Fluttering, the hardback she'd been reading

Perched like a little roof on the house
Of her chest. When I went to her, I went quietly,

Careful not to disturb the garden's foundation
Of vines, the birdbath poised on its pedestal.

What else could I do but watch her sleep?
The lives of stray hairs moving across her face.

A flicker of dream beneath her lids.
The waterless water fountain.

iv

The doctors told them, "Keep an eye
On your daughter, but she need not stay here.

Watch her take her pills three times a day.
Let her rest all day in her bedroom. But when

She descended the carpeted stairs that linked
Her world to ours, her parents said she stumbled

Like an injured angel in her nightgown down
That handful of steps and gazed about the kitchen

And its objects (the Eiffel Tower pepper shaker,
The checkered tablecloth) as if she'd entered

A stranger's house. That's when John posted
His list of chores to the refrigerator door

And Beth began to plan Mary's return to college,
The writing gig at the local paper not quite

Enough to fulfill the dean's requirements.
So came the radical, post-feminist papers

She wrote for her distance-learning course.
So came the late-night journaling sessions

That lasted well into the afternoon. *I
Am a freight train*, she wrote in perfect

Block print in a margin of a notebook. *I
Am a freight train*, she scribbled on a rolling paper.

*I am the rain. I am inane. I may not fly
Like a great blue crane, but I am not insane.*

I am not insane. I. am NOT. Insane.

V

blame the lariam blame the bad pills blame her thin blood and vanishing periods blame the spasms in her back how she could crack her neck like the snap of green twigs in flame blame the drugs they had her take blame nepal blame malaria and the faulty doctors the shrink with his bifocals and beard the mosquito for its infected proboscis blame the military for its failed recipe blame bad blood blame lucid dreams blame bellyaches and the night nurse her concoction of tablets blame linoleum blame white sheets and matching curtains breathing in and out of the window blame the ticking space heater and the stars' poor alignment western medicines' failed search for an antidote blame nausea blame vomiting blame diarrhea blame dizziness loss of balance blame stomach pain muscle pain difficulty falling asleep difficulty staying asleep difficulty   breathing blame the rash and seizures blame the rash of seizures blame rain blame the sun blame a loss of feeling in the toes confusion and forgetfulness blame the radio's bad signal blame passenger planes power lines transformers blame shaking in the arms and legs panic attacks blame hallucinations blame blame blame the parking garage's easy access blame the voices no one heard but she blame visions blame waking dreams and miscommunications blame the thoughts of suicide blame her legs that did the leaping blame the beautiful blame the mosquito its hunger blame hunger blame nepal blame the lariam blame the lariam blame anything   but me

vi

Who's to say a star-sprent sky didn't warp or flex above the foothills that night? Or that any kind of light at all broke free of the clouds to knife its gloom across the snow-banked rooftops and empty lots of Blacksburg Virginia's 3 AM? All I know for sure is the clamor the cordless made from my desk. The gin-and-tonic headache I woke to. My sister's voice like static.

This was my final semester of college, hawking Rolling Rocks and hoagies to professors and ROTC at a deli a block from the power plant. On Fridays I'd kneel in rubber gloves to cleanse the massive industry of Steakumms and Kraft powdered alfredo for an extra under-the-table five. Then I'd clock out to fight the gales of wind that gathered speed between the dormitories and halls before finding my seat around the conference table of amateur theorists.

But I have no idea what 3 AM this was or whether the westerlies howled or bayed as my sister's words caromed the complicated wound of my ear. All I know for sure is how slowly the receiver fell from my hand, the dent it left in the hardwoods, how the lights in the hallway snapped to life and my roommates floated from their bedrooms in their nightclothes like angels.

Who knows what else happened that day? I've read a platoon of American boys led a night raid on Kabul and came back men. I have no doubt the thermometers ruptured at the county airport with cold. Somewhere, it's certain, God made another of God's billion daily revisions of the world.

But what did any of that matter anymore? All I could see was you. The ledge. All that snow. Your mother clenching the blue bedsheets in her sleep. Your father holding his head in his impossible hands. The calls he has to make.

vii

That first morning, I wandered my apartment as if I'd never listened
To the warming of its foundation or the buckling of floorboards,

The wan dust and debris of everyday life
Floating in columns of daylight through the east windows.

When the train whistle cooed its sluggish way through town,
A motley crew of wintering crow lifted like paint fumes from my backyard.

When a roommate's alarm erupted, a showerhead burst to life,
And the coffeemaker kept insisting 12:00 AM 12:00 AM 12:00 AM 12:00 AM

What else is there to say? What else recall?

That first morning, it wasn't Mary that haunted me or her leap,
But her father's words, diffuse and malformed through the telephone,

That voice once so certain I held to my ear, I sat on the bed,
I did nothing, I said nothing, I did everything I could.

viii

Kicking pebbles on the shoulder of the highway,
I tested the wind's direction with a finger. The winds
That came spoke of hoarfrost and fields. Commerce
Rumbled by on I-40. The streetlamps burned
Their fishhook of light before the red-brick Victorian—
Its locked double doors, its hundred shuttered eyes.
Not a family member, not a lover, no guests welcome
Past visiting hours, I watched the night watchman doze
In his A-frame of spit cups and *Hustler*, I observed
The roosting of birds, the library of stars above the trees
That lined the county road where I drafted my path
Over the high outer wall and through the just-mown
Grass, the method by which I'd scale the sanitarium,
Tap a finger on her window, whisper, "Mary, let me in."

*

I still don't know why I've kept her so long in this house
For the somewhat-less-than-sane where they kept her
A mere 24 hours, a two-hour's drive from her bedroom
Where she hid herself the year before she died.
That December home from college, I'd park
Across the street from her house, warm my hands
By the heat of my Nissan Sentra's 4-cylinders,
And wait to catch a glimpse of Mary in her window.
More than a decade since she killed herself. Still
I don't know why. She spent a year in college.
She climbed the mountains of Nepal, helped raise schools
For the poor. In the one picture I've kept, she smiles
At the camera. Sometimes a fly catches on the glass
In the frame. Sometimes I think I catch her blink.

*

And what would you do differently? Mary asks, sights trained
Through the passenger window on that glowing square
Of light that could be the window of the imagined sanitarium,
Could be the window of her bedroom on Wyoming Ave.
She's blue-eyed here. The breeze is honeysuckle and sex.
And even though she knows I've no answers, knows
When I say nothing, I say everything, she places a finger
To my lips to freeze me in that game of *What Ifs* I've been playing
Since college then departs to follow that brick path back
To herself from the mailbox to the stoop, through
The sanitarium's arched entry past her kitchen and down
The cinderblock hallway to her bedroom while I'm stuck here,
Eyeing that figure lighting the window. A chest x-ray
Or the moon? The girl I loved? The girl I thought I knew?

A Calling

Day after day, I traverse this land, of the earth
Beneath me, I dream. Deep in the dark of the Green
River Valley: Mammoth Cave, Kentucky, and all
I have left of that seventh-grade field trip, this geode,

Mere nodule of limestone shaped like a fist my mother
Found turning out my pockets for the wash, amethyst
Amulet my father helped chisel open, its countless
Purple cyphers cracking open before us

Only to be packed away in a box in the basement
When I moved away, this artifact of a past life I found
Struggling with my classmates through a squeeze
In the cave when our tour guide rasped "Listen!"

Before toggling off the thin string of halogens
That lit our way. At first? Nothing. Only darkness
Predicated on more darkness, girls' shrieks echoing
Between the rebound and hush of nervous laughter.

Then. Quietly. Low rumblings of the river carving
Its corridors below, random drips of water, a sensation
Of a movement in the air. And the glowworms opened.
In the beginning, one by one. Then tens. Then a thousand

Frail pilot lights flaring to life, tiny and cold blue
As the eyes of newborns. There, in that acetylene aura,
We were told the tale of the classroom "just like yours"
That lost its way decades before the advent

Of the incandescent bulb, those children of the saltpeter
Mines and tobacco fields feeling their way along shelves
Of flowstone and gypsum, their pitch-pine torches slowly
Succumbed to the dark, their teacher having abandoned them

"For his own children's sake," some of the children
Weeping, some still clinging to the hope of calling out
"Mother! Father!" many disappearing "without a sound."
That first night the geode sat on my bedside,

The dream was slow coming, sleeplessness
In the broad sweep of headlights that crawled
My bedroom walls, wind howling its low frequency
Of omen and admonishment until I found myself not in bed

But holding hands with a girl my age in a pea coat and wide hat
Of the old style, shiny black shoes strapped to her feet
With silver buckles, her face lacking any detail like the way fish
Must see daylight through the silent shunt of their streams.

And when I found myself standing with her on the banks
Of that underground river swift with whitecaps
Like white tongues, I didn't think to protest when she stepped
Into the rapids and slipped away around a bend in the dark.

I don't pretend to understand it, this dream, but sometimes
I'm convinced it's about goodness. Now when it comes,
I look down at the earth scattered with a light like the light
Innate within seeds. Then I'm back in that torrent,

The cave walls sprouting river trees, carrion birds burdening
The branches of water cypress. And when this host of lost children
Calls out, I call back, and when I get it right, they rise
From the river in the form of quiet sparks, in the form

Of fallen stars as they glide through the air to enter the geode
Singing from my palms in the mother tongue of the elements,
Guided by the promise of a better place not so wet
And dark and cold and I: their keeper.

On the 1ˢᵗ Anniversary of Mary's Death

I have no words, bare feet burning with cold,
Vision hazed with waking. On the first

Anniversary of Mary's suicide, I rise to thumb
Through the glow of digital news, tap my finger

On the counter, impatient with the coffeemaker's task.
Beyond the window: the city's transit is delayed

By snow. Commuters skate across the freeway.
A traffic reporter hovers secretly above.

"It's not death that stuns our senses," I say
To the sketch of my face in the window,

"But how we depart. It's not the end
That distracts our reading," I mutter a day after

The Sabbath I still do not observe, "but how
We've lived." Mary's still out there, patrolling

The far woods. Mary's still reaching for my thin face
With her thin hands. *Listen,* she keeps saying.

Say it. After me: "There was nothing I could do."

Marysarias

> *Ghosts, too, have dreams*, she tells me—

The living and the dead
Drawn out of the mist by strange, reined beasts:

    Chimeras with the bodies of lions, the giant, croaking heads of toads,
    Oxen in tandem, winged and tailed with the flames of controlled burns.

Mary suspended in this dull talc.
No wind, no earth.
No moisture, no heat.

Light the sourceless lux of an animal's skin.
                              Sound
The stir of breath fading from windows. Echoes whisked
Through narrow corridors of brick and steel.
Wind weaving the dead, bare limbs of many dead, bare trees,

And even if she could see beyond this thick vapor and steam,
No mountains like broken teeth in the distance,
No gulls scratching their beaks against the blackboard sky,
No breakers breaking back into foam against the rock-strewn strands
      of dead oceans.

Sometimes, she's visited by family in the dream.

Her mother and father, of course. Both sisters.
                                  Once,
It was her great grandfather who peered
Through the lampblacked window of his stagecoach,
His lab coat crisp and white as creased sheets of paper—he
Who discovered the particle nature of light, he
One of 53 inventors of the atomic bomb.

Sometimes it's those who found her:

The security guard still haunted by the shape of her body
Beneath his pea-green parka, the nurse's lips still cold
With the faint pulse felt when she touched her lips to Mary's.

Other times, it's the last to see her alive:

First, a man. A young lawyer standing in his suit before his office window.
Nashville in its mid-winter husk, *BRUTON SNUFF COMPANY*
In cold neon above traffic and treeline—Mary climbing
Onto the ledge of the parking garage rooftop.

Then: a woman. Young like my mother
In the years before those snakes of gray hair dropped
From her temples, a waitress cupping a Pall Mall against the wind,
Tips singing a fire in her apron pocket—
Mary falling from the sky.

Once:
An entire caravan of Nepalese children shuttled by in the fog,
Smiling and waving as if Mary were back in the Manang Valley,
Directing these small villagers, "Squeeze in"
As she adjusts the camera's focus, the digital f-stop flipped to infinity,
The rising low clouds of the valley angled into the frame.

Sometimes, she tells me, strangers emerge from the half-light:

Flight attendants coiling their hair in buns with Number 2 pencils,
Migrants begging for work in the lot of a Home Depot,
Night janitors pushing their push brooms down the long, sterile hallways of
       their paychecks.

Sometimes, she calls out to them, but no one hears her.

     Always it ends the same, she says:

Thick braids of mist swirl about her.
Vague notion of moisture, vague notion of heat.
A presence in the drifts of dust.

Then the slow breaking apart of the self:

Frail wafts of her arm merging with the vapor,
Strands of hair drifting like dandelion heads from their roots,

Mary joining hands with the fog,
The fogged breath of God.

Once, we were two kids who should've been in love,
Carving shortcuts and jogs from the Nashville maps
As we banged our heads to Nirvana turned up full tilt
Through my Nissan-Datsun's single speaker,
So bored with the smallness of our lives
Only made smaller by our classmates who parked

Friday nights around Love Circle, downtown Nashville
Lit up below us like a deep-sea installation
In the romantic dark, exhausted condoms and the last
Backwash drags of George Dickel bottles tossed to the kudzu
In strangleholds around the city's single Cingular tower
That pulsed its red light above us all,

Both of us imagining, I imagined, what life would be
Had our parents not met before we were conceived—our sisters
Not raised like sisters—had we met, instead, in the shade
Trees of my thirteenth August or swinging in the rope-nest woven
In the high branches of the tallest magnolia of Centennial Park
Where we taught one another to haggle tall, cold
Cans of beer from the homeless for two bucks a pop,

Both of us imagining, I imagined, as we swung,
What things would be had we met stumbling
Through the dark of McCabe's 9th green,
Had we counted the stars with our backs to the hard, flat turf
Of business decisions and Dixiecrats, the pole's yellow pennant
Flapping like a heart murmur in the breeze.

She thinks she knows what it's about, the dream,
                                          but I don't ask—

For this is a dream for me as well. Who else but the dream-self
Would enter a dead girl's sleep? What else but the dream-self
Would return to this parking garage rooftop?

Mary, again 19,
The oldest age she'll ever be.

Nashville. 2003.
The first and only snow of the year
Drifting out of the clouds,

Her '95 Corolla idling nearby in its spot,
Exhaust chuffing the air with a heat
Like that of the earth released
Into the cold universe.

Dead Girl dead now seventeen years,
Dead Girl conceived beneath Sagitta, the arrow,
Delphinus, the dolphin, Cygnus, the swan,

Tell me what brings us here seventeen years after the fact,
Tell me what stuffs these hands in my vest pockets?

What calls me into the night descending
Like a mourning veil across the city?
No pedestrians, no wind.
No jets sighing overhead.

Just the white-hot glow of a glass elevator
Tracing the spine of the Renaissance Hotel—
A white-hot light rising through the deep—

The distant ant-like outlines of its passengers
Small silhouettes of Mary and me seventeen years ago,
Leaning with our foreheads pressed to the cool, curved glass

As limousines and bellboys drop away from us
And Nashville unfolds like a relief map at our feet.

From here, 40 floors above the blacktop,
The penthouse restaurant of the Sheraton twirls
Like a spacecraft from another world.

Is that Steiner-Liff, the recycling plant
Of Pontiacs and Accords stamped in slumped stacks
Of crushed steel and glass?

Is that I-40 and Briley Parkway and the Cumberland
Silently divining the city into precincts and slums,
The Tennessee Tower looming darkly

Above the state capital, the *L&C* marquee
Sizzling in the pan of night's unending hour
That tonight of all nights

Passes too slowly for the bag ladies blanched
By the street's steam grates, the lap dancers
Dangling their hair across the hard cocks of their patrons

As the crowd noise rises from the football stadium
As our quarterback toes the sideline
And all the aspiring songwriters strum
All at once their acoustics and all the listeners
Close their eyes and rise up in eulogy to Mary

As if this city, as if this network of fiber optics
And storm drains and vitrified clay piping
Was raised to sing her name,

As if, if we placed our ears to its sidewalks,
We'd hear Mary's arias beneath downtown's boulevards and one-ways,
Mary's arias within the skyscrapers
And highways and cul-de-sacs and empty lots,

Marysarias within these brick-and-mortar walls,
Marysarias in this lyric of rebar, this lyric of steel.

Tell me, Third Child,
Tell me, Third and Final Daughter slipped
So easily from the womb,

What is it really, that mineral we call moon
Candescing the sky?

At night is it a sheared half penny
Flipping end-over-end behind the blink of an eye?

By day does it speak,
Soft mumblings of the grief we carry inside us,
This grief having dropped yet again from its dark nest?

Whitewashed Harvest, Whitewashed Moon,
                                                    for what have I come?

Your hair picked up in the wind like blonde streamers of fire.
Your pelisse skirt and blouse. Your feet skin-bare
Against snowfall and frostbite.

Mary, your death is the scent of half-burned candles.
Mary, your death is the red bloodshot of a sleepless eye,

Your children who never cry out in the night,
Your children who never break the back of sleep.

Speak, Sad Child, speak.

Tell us of the lingering, the marble-eyed
Who trace silent paths through the grazing grounds of horses.

Tell us of the everlasting curled up with the underbellies of rocks
Where skinks and salamanders roost.

I've come only for a sign.

Perhaps an injured bird hopping shadow to shadow.
All the locked car doors swinging open at once.

Perhaps others who've come for the same reason:

The security guard and nurse smiling sadly when they see one another,
My sister writing a message upside down in the snow
Like a child writing backward in the breath of a bus window.

Mary, what would you have me say?

Do I tell you your father was in my wedding?
Do I tell you how fiercely I loved my wife?

Do I tell you your mother and father sold the house?
Do I describe how your mother goes through your writings

To add to each year's Christmas letter
An entry from your notebooks?

Or do I give you updates?

Donald Trump is president.
Bin Laden was buried in the salt of a secret sea.
Michael Jackson died some years ago of sleeplessness.

I have found the love of my life.
I finally have my children.

Or do I take you back to the 3 AM my sister called?
Do I show you the two policemen who entered your father's office?

Do I tell you how they stood there in the door, their blue hats
held before them like the orbs of all life and the fate of mankind grasped
in the hands of God's first clergy?

Do I show you how your mother still jolts awake in the night,
The street rushing up at her at incredible speed?

Or do we set all that aside?

Do I take the chance?
Do I find the words with which to woo the dead?

Do I whisper into your ear?
Do I touch you with both hands at once?

Do your bones feel like bones beneath cloth?
Do your bones feel like bones beneath cloth and skin?

Tell me, *please*:

Do the living slip off their clothes for the dead?

Do the dead huddle for warmth?

How, my dear, does a dead girl shiver?

There was a time when the sea was more gentle, when it did not rage
Against the land, when fish leapt from its surfaces to fin through the
lucid air.

There was a time when love could be taken in one's hand
And shaped like clay, when, if you closed your hand

Around that clay and opened it, you'd find a human heart in your hands.

In the dream, people visit me, she tells me,
                                      but you are never here.

Once we were two kids who should've been in love, she says.

In the dream, these visitors have places to go,
                                      but I cannot go with them.

Always it ends the same, she says.

I am hanging in a fog

No moisture No heat

And even if I could see beyond the mist
No mountains like broken teeth in the distance
No gulls scratch their beaks against the blackboard sky
No breakers break back into foam against the rock-strewn strands
Of dead oceans

> *There's a sound like wind weaving the limbs of dead trees*

> *There's a sound like the faint slip of breath from windows*

And then I see it

The rooftop

The children

The man in his business suit

My mother

My father

The fog

The fogged breath of God

Like the Dead

To the geese our world must be burning:
Razed, set fire to, and igneous—the earth
Below their pneumatic wings nothing more
Than a smooth sheet of ash smoothed
Across an altar. No matter how low they fly,
It's nowhere near enough, February so thick
With overcast it's as if the world were breaking
Apart and all its matter shelved in this near
Orbit of dust. Never having mapped
The moon or stars, the geese fly lost, wailing
These avatars wedged into the slug-light
Of the nightclouds, the wind and its elements
Lumed by Draco's signature snaking beyond
Reach. They call out, ghosts these geese
We can and cannot see, their cobalt-colored eyes
Scanning the drifts, wings fanning the flames
They believe flare up below. Like fish
The color of water. Like the dead. Like me.

the catalpas they shudder the catalpas they step from their roots

they lift against the heavy burden of their gravity they strain
from their bedrock stations ice shattering from their limbs that are
too many the catalpas know flood the catalpas know drought tea-tick
disease the bag worms my father once harvested from their branches

that rose behind our house to tempt brook trout and browns and though
the catalpas know nothing of the delicate dials of wristwatches
or of the singing of clocks the catalpas have authored odes to the springs
they vaguely remember that season of hours *when earth woke early*
they remind one another limb to limb that length of time

when the sun sparked something internal and their bodies broke out
in long panicles that dropped to the oracle mouths of birds proof
of their fertility and frailty alas they've delayed too long these ancient
ornamentals for signs of earth's waking alas they've waited too long
for the earth to tilt back into the sun's good graces and now they are tired

of being on hold tired of that thin telephone song winter plays
across the white landscape that season of jingles rattling the asphalt
so they wake the catalpas so they startle their endowment of February
birds they shake their many arms shed great skeins of ice as they form
their procession as they hum sans irony the lullabies that once hummed

them to sleep bursting one after the other from hardwood into yet
another urn of ash as they topple from the edge of the uni-dimensional
world roots trailing after them roots frayed and tangled as radio wires
roots gelid tentacles wriggling from the deep a comet's tail these misplaced
lovers tadpoles of light swimming toward and always away from salvation

Mare Orientale

> *Located on the far side of the moon, the impact crater*
> *known as Mare Orientale is one of the most striking lunar features...*
> —Griffith Observatory Museum, Los Angeles, CA

Imagine that lens focused back upon the man
And woman creatures, far side of the moon
Unfixed from its sidereal glance to the stars,
An impact crater at its dead center: The dead
Constricted pupil, the shockwaves of its impact:
A flayed and tallow iris. To the living
This new moon is anything but beautiful: Silvered
Suzerain narrowed to a point, bronchioled
Oracle gibbous or full, its many phases
The phased cranking open of an eye. To the suicides
It's nothing new, just another night of judgment
Casting its broad search beam through the clouds,
Frail figures briefly illuminated between this
And the last like smudges of graphite on white
Squares of paper, draped in shawls on the shoulders
Of highways, doorways warping when they
Pass through, the moon's orbit a translucent
Curve of bone the oceans and seas must follow—
And in their chorus? No augur's voice. And in
Their shoals? No lisps of lyric. Windrows merely
Windrows swept before the dunes, no speech
Innate in the sweet white clams spitting up sand
From their burrows. *Moon*: An oculus, sabled
And socketless. *Mene*: Our keeper, cragged
And craven. *Menon*: The smeltered eye of God
Turned for eternity and away from us.

Fast Freeze

This land offers little vision
Not akin to mourning: Little

League diamond beneath its sheet
Of ice, this flock of black caps

Frozen fast to the swing set's crossbar.
O lingering winter, O flock of stunned birds,

Why *must I return here?* I'd like to ask
The pines. O *Andromeda,*

O occidental dark, why *won't this boy
Let me sleep?* I'd whisper wistfully

To the night. Instead, the origami
Of my breath folds and unfolds

Its strange memories before me: First,
The ledge. Then, bathing

With my sisters. My father
Tying a fly. My mother's face lit

By a reading lamp. Senior prom.
Unbuttoning a boyfriend's shirt

The banging of my heart.

Ice

I suppose he's forgotten that winter ice
Descended on our fair county,
For three weeks a wintry mix of hail and sleet and ice rain

Muting the boom of big rigs and tankers
That rattled past his bedroom window.

Eighteen days of subteen temperatures
And the solenoid click of dead car batteries.

Three hundred sixty hours of softball-sized hail and cumulonimbus
Making hush the rush of commuters who dreamed
Their ways home to the Whites Creeks and Mt. Juliets
That satellite our border.

A near month of snow days and bleak sky
Transformed the Nashville International Airport
Into a roosting place for "downed birds,"
The waterfront's cluster of courthouses and honkytonks
Gone dark.

It's all still there.

The bypass. His bedroom.

Mr. Forte's tithing of scrapheap Fords
Sunk to their lug nuts in the subsoil, the thirty-year elm
Still the monolith of his backyard. Everything
But the ice that turned to slush
When the cold fronts thinned and thunderheads
Broke apart into countless waxen rags,

And Nashville, our hometown, Music City,
The city of our conception, the city of our births

Became a mud-sucked wallow,

A slurry of slush and downed alders and hawthorns clogging
The city's subsystems of storm drains and catch basins,

The water tables rising as raw sewage gurgled up the galvanized
Service lines and basement drains, flock

After flock of stunned starlings
Aswirl in the eddies of the water main
To short out the sump pumps,

The tributaries and feeders slogged with debris,
Gutters sagging with the weight of thaw from their eaves.

That storm took eight lives, and it fooled us, the sun
When the storm clouds scalloped and thinned at midday

And that fiery icon appeared to ignite
All the ice-licked water towers and steeples on the hills,
And we'd think, *Perhaps this is it.*

Perhaps this is the end of all this windburn and slant hail.
Perhaps these inky nebulae will finally lift like lids
From the firmamented world and we will be free again

Only to watch the ice briefly thaw
Only to watch the ice fold back over onto itself
And freeze yet again like the process of the refinement
Of good steel, the sun's rays burnishing

All the more impassable (with its dry rag and spittoon
With its too-few plows and nowhere-near-enough salt)
Nashville's jumbled grid of surface roads and arterials,

The high rises and honkytonks and high-end hotels
Shuttered without power on the western edge of the waterfront.

———————————

Home . . . Milk-glassed metropolis . . .
Capital City so proudly brandishing your inked star, how
Could he forget all the hardwoods ice took down?

American beech and persimmon.
Hard-stoned olives and river birch.
Smooth-trunked hornbeams
And spiny-barked honey locust.

What of the green ash whose winged fruits once spun down
In thick layers beneath spring's scarred ecliptic?

What of the sycamores who once gazed upon themselves
In the purling channels of the Cumberland
And who sighed when ice felled them,
Antheming woeful narratives like paper-lipped oracles
As they drifted downriver—

Their snapped limbs the teeth of a death machine,
Their snapped limbs churning the bottleneck's rapids?

Mrs. Forte's prized chinaberry was the first
On his street to fail—a mere three days of ice
When its taproot must have snapped
And it swooned into the arms of Harvey Tanker's
Dual Wych elms and was held there half the night
Like a bride (like a mistress like a concubine)

Until the Wych elms creaked and groaned and called out
Into the night as they collapsed into a hunchbacked
Sweetgum which (like allied slavic nationhoods
Like a domino set aside another domino) toppled too

And he was shaken awake by the reverb of thunder
And the cracking of dry bones and a shudder
In his bedroom walls when his father burst
Through the door and pulled him from bed,

Dragged him by the collar down the stairs
To the basement where his mother and sister huddled
Beneath a workbench, their faces flashing
In and out of the dark until the power finally failed.

Power failures spread well beyond the county line
That night, and Word-of-Mouth spread in our dreams.

And with it, Panic spread wide its millipede arms
To embrace the many Children of God
Who made their way to Panic in their sleep.

And with Panic, the Wolf Moon clicked open,
At first no more than a pinpoint of light,
Then rippling outward like the widening aperture

Of an eye until (pale as an orb weaver pale
As an artifact archived in a box in a warehouse
Of larger boxes) it beamed in the clear sky (only clear
When full-dark rose) where it hung
And was howled to and was worshipped,

Wolf Moon who snoozed all day beneath the folding
Banquet tables of the Relief Tents stocked
With the candles and canned goods our mayor
Would hang his reelection on,

Wolf Moon who growled from his manged coat,
Spit cankered in tiny white grins about his muzzle
(tail lopped off testicles swinging between
his haunches like a hangman's noose),

Wolf Moon who stepped into the street in front
Of his father in the guise of two men knuckling
Tire irons, Wolf Moon whose teeth gleamed dully

In the cheap, Chinese-made steel of tire irons
Held in a fist, Wolf Moon who woke him
Before sunrise the night of felled trees (his crazed
eye like a looter's flashlight through the
basement windows), the hazed chord
Of his fogged breath drawing him down the hall

(as my family slept on the floor)
(as i drew pinwheels in the plumes of their hazed
breath that hung in the cold) (as i watched
the pinwheels spiral like ferrises in the gloom)

And when he found himself crawling through
The broken glass of his backdoor, he found
Himself climbing into the limbs of trees,

The branches brittle as glass
(brittle as jawbones dug up in the yard brittle as chert),

And when they broke in his hands
(i wore no gloves i wore no coat)
He spread his arms to fall and was held suspended there,
Bobbing in the dark in the limbs of fallen trees,

And when his hand fell upon a nest of dead Opossum,
His scream echoed as though he were in a chamber,

And when his hands fell upon a frozen cardinal,
He cupped that little avian in his palms
And blew into the space between thumbs like a whistle
Until he felt it twitch and unfurl

(its heart firing up like a v-twin in my hands
its lungs catching fistfuls of air like a set of pistons)

Until he opened his hands and it burst forth
From his palms, and he rose with it (and we circled
my backyard we circled my father's crushed moped
we circled the ice-entombed steeple across the street

and the circle widened as we circled
as we circled as we circled)

Until he found himself, three years in the future
On his bike, speeding down Charlotte Ave.
Toward Pearl Cohn High, backpack slung over his shoulder,
Wind cutting across his scalp as he passed his parent's bank
And passed through the grafitied throat of the underpass
To weave the maze of "Affordable" Housing,
Their foundations cracking like Pop Rocks and soda,
Toy drums and carriages and deflated footballs
Left out in the mudyards, and he circled the alleys
Between houses where garbage men fed refuse
Into the government-blue mouths of trash trucks

And he watched himself, an eighth-grader, making his way
To the abandoned quarry on the eve of his teens

(and i watched myself stand on its edge in the total dark)

(and i couldn't breathe for those seconds that seemed
like hours as i watched myself step off the quarry's edge
into the void) (and it seemed like days until i heard
myself splashdown in the bilge water [as we circled

as we circled] and i feared for my life [as the cardinal
grew impatient as we circled] as i waited for the sound
of my sputtering to the surface and swimming slowly
back to shore [as we circled as we circled as we circled])

And he circled the pea-gravel roof of Bass Junior High
And saw Laticia Moore pull him, not yet twelve, to her
Beneath the eastern stair to teach him to French kiss

As his mother checked her watch in the parking lot
As she listened to NPR, waiting yet again
To pick her son up from basketball practice,

And he saw himself in a circle of classmates
As he circled with Larry Hendrix (the white kid whose clothes
were never washed the white kid who the black kids called
white trash) just days before the summer

Between sixth and seventh grade, the circle calling
(as we circled) for one of them to throw the first punch
(as i whispered to him *you don't have to do this*)
The circle crying out for them to *stop being pussies*,

To *fight fight fight fight* and he circled (as we circled)
The storm drain's mouth and found himself, barely ten,
wriggling through its narrow slot to navigate by flashlight

Its drainpipes and intakes where white girls (it was said
by white boys) were said to come here with black boys
To fuck in the dark (as i circled as i circled as i circled).

———————————————

Oh city,

Oh little nation,

Oh small market of selective memory and quarterback
Controversies, how long it took for the I-65 to reopen,

How long it took for the salt trucks on loan from Louisville
And Cincinnati to clear your beloved network of highways

And surface roads depends on who you ask.

Three weeks of no TV.
No *Dallas* reruns on the boobtube.
No McNeill/Lehrer on the squawkbox.

No artificial heat for eighteen days.

Three-hundred sixty hours of D-Cell radios
And canned beans. Four-hundred thirty-two
Thousand seconds of hunger.

Ask Robert Leidick (the fat kid on my block
who failed the fifth grade and whose mom
stashed the stack of playboys we plundered
beneath her s-10's bucket seat) and he'll swear
We couldn't play Donkey Kong all winter.

Inquire of the Forte's next door (the good catholics
who built the home i slept in the good samaritans
who spent their saturdays at the st. mary's shelter

and scolded me for emulating magic johnson's
skyhook [*you know why* they replied when i asked])
And they'll tell you the church held services
By candlelight in the gymnasium well over a month.

Speak to his father and he'll tell you they heated
Their bedrooms by pump stove for no less than two weeks.

Talk to his mother and she'll thumb through her calendar
To discover the schoolyear was extended well into June.

Look it up and history will claim the storm lasted all
Of three days.

No declaration of natural disaster.
No rattle of John Deere generators.

No bug zapper buzz of arc lights illuminating the Relief Tents.
No Wolf Moon or looters howling through hoarfrost.

Sometimes, when silence falls like the silence
All that ice brought with it, he wonders if it ever ended:

The bypass closed down, the absence of limbs
For the wind to cut through.

More than once he's woken to the echo
Of the scrape of plows finally clearing the street in his ears
Though the chuck and growl of the window unit,
Though sunlight in slats through the Venetian blinds
Inform him it's any season but winter.

Sometimes he swears he can hear his mother
And father still arguing about the Clintons in the kitchen,
A thin crease of strained light seeping beneath his bedroom door.

That storm was seventeen years ago
(i must say before rising).

In eight years (i remind you), the girl you've always loved
Will climb to the roof of one of Nashville's buildings and vanish.

They'll say I jumped. They'll say *Mary is dead.*
Some will draw pictures of my body crippled on the sidewalk.
Some will take photos of me there, only to burn the negatives.
You'll never see Mary again, they'll say. *You must learn*

To forgive yourself. Seven years after that, my love,
Seven years after that, dear city in which we both were born
(don't say i didn't warn you), seven years after that,
Stunned abattoir of failed altos and flaming guitar picks

(rubbing the cold out of my arms gazing across
Your alleys and trash bins and smokestacks from this rooftop
[as i blink in the bright lights of the twenty-first century])

Seven years after that the floods (will come
[the floods will come] the floods) will come.

when the spires of these high rises at last darken

another day ends, another night begins, another night of doves
whistling from their icy perches, night of rats skittering
across the rooftop's ledge until the sun, until the orange moon,

until that infected boil of a helium burn sparks to life
our dark horizon and another night ends, and another day
begins, day of failed auditions and AM hangovers, day
of legal briefs and stars turning over in their graves

until the spires of these high rises at last darken
and the shadow of this parking garage pans across
the highway and up into the unholy hills, the lights above
unleased offices flickering on like little souls,

another day ends, another night begins, another night of doves
whistling from their icy perches, night of rats skittering
across the rooftop's ledge until the sun, until the orange moon,

until that infected boil of a helium burn sparks to life
our dark horizon and another night ends, and another day
begins, day of failed auditions and AM hangovers, day
of legal briefs and stars turning over in their graves

Salvation

No, no need to tell me nothing's here in this creek
But ice. No Jesus bugs walking on water.
No trout passing in and out of shadow like strangers

Exchanging graves. But I've got to believe in something
This January before the sun dissolves
Into the earth's eastern edge like the eye of a lamb

In the belly of a crow. I've got to believe that someday
I'll reach across the water and some semblance
Of a hand will pass over, that, someday, I'll catch

The reflection of my eye in ice. I will wait a long time
If I must. I will learn how a snake sheds its skin.
I will wash each daybreak with an exquisite elixir

Of river rocks and sand, and if this day
Does not end, will answer the dormant carp's prayer
By tapping my nails on the ice. I will speak

In strange custom to those crossing the burning
Of the fields. I will tell them *I am your god*,
And they will speak to You no more.

i shiver

                in warm coats i shiver to keep cold i shiver
from the center of my body and hard bones yes i shiver
when i'm not shivering under the heat of the sun i shiver in
eels of snow sweeping the street i shiver like a radiator losing
its heat to damp rooms of wet clothes i shiver like a god
relegated to a cubicle i shiver i rub my ears i rub my hands i
rock back and forth my shivering self still my cheeks are the
red of a crow's split tongue still i shiver god knows why but i
shiver my oracle hands waving above barrel fires sleeping on
street grates pedaling my wares i shiver just trying to pass the
time shiver when the living are most warm when the living
are most cold i shiver because i shiver in city streets i shiver
like the cold itself a kit fresh from the womb as i wander the
countryside i knew in life as i wander with the ice scattering
across the blacktop of my vision i shiver for shivering's sake
i shiver to know i'm still shivering i shiver as i wander as i
wonder what keeps me so cold what keeps bringing me back
to this rooftop why do the living keep speaking my name

I Too Grow Tired of Winter

Tired of cold and no snow,
Tired of this rooftop, my life now of ice

Hardened over more ice
And time, as ever, without end.

I too grow tired of the nightsmoke ever-lifting
From gutter-grates, tired of the crepe myrtles

And live oaks stunted in rows
Along 7th Avenue and Broad,

Tired of the Cumberland I've witnessed flood
And crest and flood again from this high vantage point,

A cotton slip of fog hovering above the barges,
This bunched and bundled lifeline dividing the city.

And what of the sun afloat in its chalice of sky?

And what of the moon,
The hard-boiled center of some other land
Vanquished long ago?

―――――――――――――――――

How long must I wake yet again to this rooftop?

How long must I rise to this high terrace
Of pre-paid parking spots and frozen rain
Where days pass endlessly and night
Is always the same?

Again, the 2nd Avenue Methodist
Quotes its sorrow on the hour.

Again, the streetlights click on
Like dull fluorescents above portraits in a gallery,

The arena's ring of blue arc lamps
Buoyed by the fog of the riverbank
As the thrum of rush hour grows dim,

The billboards and office buildings gleaming white
With the white light of the moon, always the same moon:
Two-quarters full and only
                    just-risen.

What else can I say of this failed city?
Of this failed life?

What else of my mother who still weeps into her hands,
My father who still blames himself?

There's a strange sort of truth in these starlings that rise
From their perches, spiraling and always in unison this flock
Shepherded by silence.

Still, I am haunted by the blank space of my name
To be filled in at the morgue, the gnawed cuticles
Of the coroner's hands.

Still, I am haunted by the phone calls my father still has to make,
The distant ringing of a cordless in the background,

My sisters the only passengers on their redeyes bound for home
That night over fifteen years ago, lap belts securely fastened

As their dark municipalities drop away from them:

Chicago sinking into the blue canvas of Lake Michigan,

The HOLLYWOOD marquee growing smaller and smaller in the window
Like the bold-capped letters of a seeing eye chart.

Every night
I follow memory the many miles from this rooftop to my home.

Every night
I slink the brick walkway from the mailbox to the stoop.

I pass through the keyhole, I slip beneath the door.
I sit in the kitchen counting the seconds until morning
When daylight turns the blinds into blinding parallels.

In the dark I riffle curtains
Only to watch them smooth themselves back to order.

In shadow I remove all the novels and neatly-accordioned maps
From their spots on the shelves
And place them on their faces on the floor like tarot

Only to watch them open their spines, test
Their paper wings, and flutter back to their designations
Between bookends.

Night after night,
I practice fourth-notes and fifths on the baby grand.

Always it ends the same:

My mother startling awake from sleep,
My father certain "it's her" practicing scales a floor below
Like I did in life,

And just as they turn the corner in their nightclothes,
                                                    I vanish

All over again.

More than fifteen years since I leapt from that ledge.
More than fifteen years since I took my leave of one world
only to awaken into this one.

Same landmarks. Same moon. Same rush hour
And scarred trees and nightbirds calling out,
Same voices rising from the street
But not a single human soul, not a single human body
                                        connected to them.

That first night, I peered down from the ledge
To see my carbon-copy self
Seven stories below, a mute form beneath a man's coat, the man
Nowhere to be found.

And now your appearance each winter in your jacket and boots.
And now, over a decade expired, your pacing back and forth
From the satellite dish to the ledge
                        and back again,

Speaking to the air and sketching images in your notebook
With trembling hands:

"the old coat of arms on the cornice of a building across 7th"
"a green desk lamp making light in an eighth-story window"

Other words for darkness, winter, fog, synonyms
For grief, "Speak, Sad Child, speak" scribbled,
Marked out, then circled several times with a note to self
In the margin: "THIS. YOU. KEEP."

Every night, once the sun is full gone,
I descend from this rooftop and take

To the empty highways. I wander the countryside
Our fathers believed would save us.

I hold my arms deep in frigid water until they burn.
I traverse the frozen creeks, careful not to crack their glass roofs.

I know how each night's journey will end
Before I even descend from the rooftop.

I know that no matter how far I wander,
No matter what words I form into what prayer,

The same sun always turns the corner
And night ends with that telltale tug at my shoulders

And I am lifted from the earth
And pulled back the way I have come,

The cold silos and well-lit highways I've only
Just journeyed through passing swiftly beneath my feet,

The fiery light of the suburbs boiling the horizon,
The cityscape of vacated condos and glowing complexes

Of high-rises and light climbing the curve of the earth
And I am back, yet again in this city of dreamers.

———————————

Listen.

This wasn't what I had in mind, this rooftop.

I did all I could to exit this life.

I did not intend this ledge I leap from each day like a chore.

Why have you damned me to this endless winter?

I'd ask if I had a voice. *Why won't you allow*

the American robins and cedar waxwings their return?

I repeat and repeat in his ear.

If God were a thing I had faith in,

I'd place my hand across my heart and stand up straight.

If God were a pair of wind-up teeth left here by a child,

I'd set God on this ledge and watch God chatter to the brink.

If God were anything at all, I'd say *Return*.

I'd say, *Take me there.*

I'd ask, *Why.*

Why won't this boy let me rest?

Why won't you let me sleep?

Night

Is all muskiness and raven wings,
The dangerous whir of box fans

And caterwauling window units,
My alarm clock on the bed stand

Bright as a flare. Down the hall,
My mother and father sleep fitfully

As crows and my sister in her basement
Bedroom of wood-paneling still

Hasn't hung up the telephone.
So I step out my upstairs window,

Careful as a mime not to crack
The green shingles flecked

With coughed-up stars. I feel
My way along the roof to the cherry

Laurel, make sure not to wake
The mutt yoked to a rusty eye-bolt

And chain as I make my way
To the cohort of elder boys

Who wait in the alley in the green
Buzz of Newports, skin made alien

By saccharin streetlamp light.
In the middle of this life, I woke

To find myself: A mass of aching
Molars and sun-bruised skin, grit

In my teeth from chewing my nails.
Back then scabs turned to a gelatinous

Film in the chlorine of the city pool,
No one strayed past Charlotte and 32nd

Avenue past dark, and when a boy
Like me turned thirteen, he ventured

To the quarry on the midnight
Of his birth, the quarry, legend told,

Abandoned generations ago
On the corner of Woodrow Wilson

And Park, the quarry, it was rumored,
The massive socket of an unearthed

Grave where boys my age must go
In the sodden, midnight ether of April,

A little early for the fourth night
Of the fourth month of the 94th year

Of the 20th Century, the quarry,
They say, a religion, a greed,

An alluvial spirit, a history of boys
Found belly-down in its too-shallow

Waters. The quarry belongs.
The quarry is stoic. The quarry

Giveth and the quarry *taketh away*,
A black circumference encircled

By shot-gunned warning signs
In white bold, the quarry the center

Around which the maze
Of my neighborhood spirals,

The axis of that blazing wheel
Of high tops and work boots dangling

From telephone wires, the swollen
Lobe of an ear pierced by an infected

Zirconia stud at Bass Junior High,
The quarry the pupil of pinkeye,

The progeny of strays no one bothers
To catch though they growl

With hunger and with their longing
As they doze in the shadow

Of my grade school's sheet-metal
Auxiliary, the quarry is the dog

Shit you scrape from your sneakers,
Pickup games beneath the bent

Double-rims of desire, footnotes
Of urine winging across the singed turf

Of churchyards and government
Asphalt. *At least you're fed,*

The quarry says, *At least you lived*
This long, it muses while buffing

Its mile-long thumbnail
With the pages of a *Barely Legal*.

On the short walk there, I kick
A crushed soda can down

The alleys limned with failed
Streetlamps. When I arrive,

I shimmy like a thief beneath
the fence rimmed with razor wire,

I stand reverent before the darkness
of the vacuum that drops away

Before me. *Your life is not your own*,
A single dove coos from its tree.

You you you are going to *die die die*,
It clucks from its dowry of wings:

Faggot, Cumslut, Momma's Boy
Just a few of the terms I will

Continue to endure if I do not
Jump, no matter the drought year,

No matter the foretelling
Alignment of planets, no matter

My mother's cracked hands,
Her impatiens drooping in their hotbed.

"It's time," I must mutter
To myself like heroes in the movies.

The quarry is no more than an echo
Before me. The boys who urge

Me forth are huddled in half-circle
Behind. Can you see how each

Of them mutes a flashlight
In their palms? Can you see

How each of them offers their heart
To the muscular dark?

Far from the Fields Turned Crystalline by Winter

Far from Februaries that mean all but the Tennessee cedars
And loblollies stripped down to their frail cores,
                                                        the dead keep quiet.

In the eerie half-light and chill of my first winter in Los Angeles
The dead remain disfigured, the Pacific's lukewarm lilt
So alien to the frozen ponds and frost-limned creeks I've left behind,

This great grid of smokestacks and accosted dreams
Tossed like a seine net from my apartment window,
My reflection its own sentient being in the glass.

Still, though I look, no sign of Mary
In this fragile network of asphalt and waterworks and desert.

West of the salt flats, just east of the sea itself:
No sign in the San Gabriel's cycle of burn and snowcap,
                                                              snowcap and burn.

In the dark's brittle tincture . . .
In the twelve-story shadow cast by my apartment building . . . .
On the 10th anniversary of Mary's death . . . ,

   Mary is nowhere to be found.

Her name in Latin means "a Star of the Sea,"
                                                  the Wished-for Child.

Its root in Hebrew means bitterness and rebellion—
Mary the girl who had a way with flightless things.
Skipping stones worked their way into her pockets.
Box turtles dropped from their logs in the sun and dogpaddled ashore.

Once, she bought a treasure trove of keys
From an antiquarian at the County Fairgrounds

And kept them at all times on a ring
To test locked doors we did not know.

The first time it worked, we were in a museum
Of natural history. The door we secreted open

Opened onto row after row of animal parts afloat
In the glow of chemical solutions: a raccoon's paw bobbing

In formaldehyde, a rhesus monkey brain
Coiled in saline buffers and Magnesium chloride.

The second time, she balanced a bronze doorknob
On an anthill, slipped a key into its tumblers,

And a light burst forth
From a crack in the earth—

Mary the girl known for the most simple of ingenious designs:
The language of hand signals and flags we used

From tree house to tree house in my backyard, a whistle
From a stalk of grass, her bird trap

Nothing more than a cardboard box
Propped open with a stick.

That box beat from within like a fussy child on a changing table
As Mary wrapped it in butcher paper and twine,

And I doubt she'll ever forget her disappointment
When we presented our gift of captured flight

To the bag lady who lived in the alley behind my house—
How she failed to transform like the myths

We read to one another by nightlight
From our book of myths:

   That old lady no more than an old lady,
   Our book of myths a book of myths.

———————————————

Mary knows I've left behind the city of our births.
She can smell the singe and caust- of Manifest Destiny.
She has watched the sun's sodium ray ascend the San Gabriels
Like the inverse of ink on cotton.

Still, no matter how early I wake,
Daylight fractures into countless renderings of itself across the Pacific
And all I see of her is in nightmare:

Every night, the phone's rattle at 3 AM,
   my sister on the other end with the *terrible news*.

Every night, snow dropping in perfect white verticals
   to make a barcode of my window in Virginia.

Every night, the word suicide made real:
   This lump in my throat, this image of the girl I so loved
Falling from the sky.

So I say her name aloud in public places:

Mary on my daily walk into the enormity of the city,
Drifting crowd to crowd, always further from home than the day before
Where I buy my breakfast from a street vendor
And squat on the curb in the hopes she'll materialize
From the scuff of work boots and petroleum,

Mary traveling north on the subterranean corridors of the Blue Line,
The pale cup of her face unblinking in breakaway glass,

Mary beneath my breath in a sold-out theater,
The stage with its trapdoors, the players in their slack-jawed masks.

Sometimes, I try *Rebellion*
As I slip my bus fare into its slot.

Sometimes, I plea *Sorrow, Indignation, Wished-for Child*
As I wander the portraits and landscapes in a gallery.

Back home, I could find her in forsythia's first blooms,
Could draw her face in salt spilled on the bar of my favorite watering hole.

Back home, I could take myself to the shortcut she fashioned
From three underpasses, a handful of alleys, and the parking lot

Of the nursing home on Broadway and 5th
And find her waiting for me in her front yard.

Here, when I write Mary's name in the dust
Of my bedroom window, she takes a step back.

Here, with each day that passes,
The distance between us swells.

Maybe it's not the dead who linger
but the living they leave behind,

These ghosts of who we once were
Scouring the creek beds and ditches
In the darkling fields on the other side of the road
As we seek out the past,

Remnant and fragmentary, lost and found
                                                  and lost again.

So I make my appeal to this City of Angels
   and personal demons.

So I give voice to my desires
   in this hour of neon and streetwalkers.

So I say *rise*. So I say *return*. And I wait.

Meditation on Balsam Mountain

The stars are so numerous tonight, I've nearly lost myself
Connecting them: Virgo barely risen from the heat-weak
Horizon, the great bear all but invisible against its milky smear.

Somewhere below these loci of brilliant light, somewhere
Beyond the earth's backward bow, there's a certainty and silence
To be found, a purpose and answered prayer. Yet, when the sun

Reappears, the barred owls will be wise to halt their questioning,
The mountain lions will catch a scent they dare not follow.
If I knew the way to the life of such wild things, I'd go there:

The evergreens' constant shift, a razor-edged escarpment
Through a pass, wings banging against the moon. But no matter
How many times I dream of not waking, I do. No matter

How many times I rehearse the proper words, they all
But spill from my mouth. *Come, show me the way*,
I demand of Polaris's burning heart. *Come*

Finish what you started, I mouth to nothing and no one,
Yet again having counted the stars on this bald peak,
Yet another unnamed and nameless hour ticking into the next.

The Lost

Look, there, where all the lost children stand:

Hands stuffed in pockets, embarrassed
And a little bit shy as they toe the surf, the ocean
A blue sheet of paper pulled back and forth from the beach
By steel cables.

How long must they wait there, huddled together,
Keeping away from the tide? How long
Must they wonder where they are, waking each morning
By the strange bemoanings of the inland forest,
The waterline punctuated with bodies?

Some of them look back and forth at one another's faces
And ask the questions without answer:
How did we get here? Do you know your name?

Some of the children drag the dead from the sea
By their armpits, shallow trenches heeled
Behind them in the sand.

The rest peer out when the sun first releases
Its heat, hands lifted to their brows as if to salute
The ocean rippling before them like a carpet beat by a broom.

I think they hope to see me, dangling just inches
Above the waves on the far horizon.

I think they think I am a ship bound for their harbor,
Some strange species of bird come to save them.

I think they think I know what I'm doing,
Shuttling back and forth across their field of vision,
Hair rising from my scalp like a bed of snakes.

But this is not what I had in mind when I leapt
From that building—inflamed
Whatever place this is like a nail-bit cuticle, swollen
This skyline infected with pink eye.

The sun's logic spins inside out as it slides west
To east along the hard horizontal of the horizon.
These notions of who I once was reach for me from the beach.
The sky of brushed steel blisters my teeth.

A Brief History
of the Living World

Rise, *she says*. Rise,
You fieldstones. Rise
As if from some
Great toil. Rise from
Your constrain of earth,
From my constant
Onus of Feldspar
Of Chert of Quartzite.

O Hornstone, O basalt
Of my dreams,
She mutters, you are
Blessed—canker
Of my father's lawn
Mower, everyday
Element of the Io
Moon. O whin-

Stone, how you
Flash your dun colors
From the streambed
Most beautiful
When cresting its high
Watermark,
The inflammation
Of Venus shifting
Across the surface. O

Menonite,
How acutely you fit
Into my rock-smoothed palm,
These lands made barren
By my scavenging,

By the dreams
Of the breathing,
Quickened by the dawn
Of the second guess,
The 20/20 visionary. Rare

These days to find
Even a knuckle bone
Of Sandstone of Shale
Of crystallized Safflorite
Pressed by freeze
And thaw and by
The intense, irrational sun,
The soft surfaces of these
Hills once roamed
By cum-heavy bulls,

These slopes once
Jagged, these steppes
Once rigid and spired
Now smooth
As the likeness
Of a concubine's
Rouged cheeks
As the backbones
Of golden spoons
As strands
Of my still
Elegant hair.

Now these lands
Are all Schist all Silt-
Stone all Slate. No
Tonality in the sea
Breeze. No wonder
In the night tasteless

As an unsalted Borscht
Full of the cries
Of the child
I never made. Yet

Still I come to gather
What Obsidian
What Iron what handfuls
Of Anthropolite I
Can muster. Still
I compose these
Cairns of stone
When their corpus
Becomes too great
A burden, these cairns
Dotting the mountainside
Like bits of redacted code.

Bluestone, Mica-
Bossed, Pumice: No
One thinks to thank
You for molding
The hard palates of
Newborns,
For shaping the hard
Shapes of consonants
And glottal stops. Coal,

Granite, Alabaster:
No one thinks to sing
Your praises
When they pray,
Such words reserved
For whatever gods
They believe
One day will reveal
Themselves.

No one knows what I'm
Doing here, *she says*.
Least myself.

Sometimes I believe
I'm clearing the fields of their hard
Makings, smoothing
The rutted, ravaged earth
Into a paradise. Heaven-
Maker, I ought to call
Myself, *she says*, Levigator-

By-Hand of the ridge-
Lines more ancient
Than this now expert eye
Scanning the waste
For whatever Ore, Marble,
Bitumen jigs up
From the engine
Of whatever it is
That churns this boiling
Plane of Ash of Salt
Of Clay and Burned Grass
Despite my constant
Labors—the city a dull pulse
Beyond the hills,
The city the electric eye
Of the stove my grandmother
Always worried she'd
Left burning. O

What I wouldn't give
For some rest
Without dream. O

Who I wouldn't provision

For some peace:
No longer this silent
Call to ardor, no
Longer this image
Cast before me
Of myself muttering

These words
To myself when,
On occasion,
Like a spark, like a flash
Of the instant,
I eye some prize
In the parched, dun dust
And drop

With exhaustion
With relief
With need
To my knees
To present whatever gem
I've uncovered
To the thunder-
Lit sky—some find
Beyond sand, beyond yet
Another newborn's
Unclaimed molars, perhaps

Hematite perhaps Soap-
Stone perhaps some
Other invaluable prize
Of the living world
I thrust into the wind-
Loud heavens. "Rise,

Maker of stone," I say.
Rise, Creator, Destroyer
To heave and pulsate
And thunderclap
Your approval your
Opprobrium your final
Desire, and I
Will give it.

Say something more
Than this dead quiet.

Have the gall to finish
What you've started.

Speak, *she says*. Speak,
She says. Speak, *she*
Says, she says, she says.

On the 10th Anniversary of Mary's Death

We're supposed to return to this place of ledges
And pressure-washed parking spaces, low and labored
Winter clouds, the shadows of high rises. Sky. On the tenth
Anniversary of Mary's death, we're supposed to return here
—I, my mother, my father; I, her mother, her father.
We're suppose to drop by on impulse from our workdays
Of high schoolers and familial obligations on the same day
And in the same weather, having donned the same raiment
And holding forth the same dour portraits of our faces
As echoes rise from the one-way seven stories below: A baby
Wailing her hunger sirens from her stroller perched on the curb,
The homeless man busking for change on the corner,
The orange-vested workman singing down his commandments
From the basket of the Nashville Electric Company cherry picker.
On the tenth anniversary of Mary's death, we're supposed
To meet here unplanned. No communiqués from this seven-
Story terrace of parking spots and freezing rain. No emails.
No time and place encoded in a text. On a Wednesday, sad
Middle child of the five-day workweek, perhaps. Or the 23rd
Of August, that most arbitrary of dates. Maybe that extra 24 hours
Tacked on to the Leap Year—no matter the date, the same
Effluvia of the slow river, of trash rotting in gutters,
Of rotting teeth, the same blood of the same fish wafting up
From the waterfront as I—my mother, my father—as I—her mother,
Her father—ascend the dim stairwells on our opposite corners
Of the garage, straining to make the climb to the roof
Where we're supposed to arrive a bit dazed by the sudden blaze
Of daylight through the roof-access doors we haul open
And step through into the glare of 3 PM, 10 AM, just before dark.
On the tenth anniversary of Mary's death, there's supposed
To be that moment when we eye one another across the oily
Aegean of brightly-colored pickups and sedans, followed
By that moment when we see one another and watch
Each other's mouths form the same words, "Who the fuck

Is that?" before the next moment jigsaws into place
And our faces unknot their confusion and we recognize each other
All at once, and we all know at the same time
That we've come to the same place for the same reason.
None of us smiles or waves as we come together at the rooftop's center.
No one says anything at all. On the tenth anniversary
Of Mary's death, we're supposed to arrive alone,
Just the five of us—I, my mother, my father—I,
Her mother, her father—to form a crude elliptical of breathing.
No one is supposed to say any of the logical things—
"How are you?" "Where is she?" "How did you know?"—
As we peer into each other's eyes, and in much the same way
A charged ion must see through the scope of a ground wire,
We see into each other's pupils and down into the blue maps
Of aortas and down all the way through sinew and bone
Into the all-too-easily-bruised heel of the foot.
Mary, in that moment, is supposed to appear, listening
With her ears to the words lipping from our mouths
As she presents us with comforting words that scroll
Like white subtitles across the dark scripts of our minds.
Here, today, she's supposed to touch us. An ear lobe.
An elbow. The backs of the knees. She's supposed
To be giving us back something taken away.
And when it's time, she's supposed to slink back into the cracked
And weathered pavement like a drying up creek bed,
Like a shadow slowly losing its light source. And we're supposed
To break our council and disperse from this place more than a decade
After Mary's death by whatever ways we've come—by bus,
By the tangled web of avenues, by the cool cylinder of a 737—
And we're supposed to no longer wake from dreams
Of Mary still alive only later to remember she is dead
And grieve all over again. We're supposed
To work regular hours for a living and pay the bills
On time and sing along to the hymns of Mick Jagger
Without turning to sorrow and remember to call our elders "Sir"
And "Ma'am" and recall more memories more fondly

And actually take note when a street changes names
And remember the name and no longer get so damned lost
On the way to the grocery or Target, lost in that memory
Of that tiny eatery in Odessa so full of song that burned like a little bell
Just drop forged on the black Black Sea in the days before Mary
Was no longer herself. "What was it called?" we're supposed
To one day wonder aloud to ourselves above the steering wheel.
"The Mamacasalla? The Little Cosmonaut? The girl
Who worked there, the prostitute you didn't realize
Was a prostitute until you failed to pay for a kiss? What was her name?
I think she called herself Isabella. Or was it Elena?
Or were we in Helsinki? Or Budapest? America?" Who knows
For sure who she was? Who knows for sure where we were?
Who knows for sure who any of us are?

On the 100ᵗʰ Anniversary of Mary's Death

> *We were neurophobic and perfect*
> *the day that we lost our souls*
> *Maybe we weren't so human*
> *But If we cry we will rust*
> *And I was a hand grenade*
> *That never stopped exploding*
> *You were automatic and as hollow as the "o" in god*
>
> "Mechanical Animals," Marilyn Manson

No, no notice arrives in the mail. No, we do not convene above her body in a smaze of visitation and candlelight. Her casket is not raised on a castered granite slab. My hands do not grip its stone-cold edge. The cold jewels of Mary's eyes do not flap open in the dark. Mary's cold hands do not press against her coffin's velvet ceiling. Mary's mouth does not open into a scream.

No, on the one-hundredth anniversary of Mary's death, we do not form a procession of SUVs and sedans to rattlesnake our right-of-way through the flooding of the city. We do not flash our headlights past boarded-up courthouses and nail salons. There are no grocery carts constellatory in the abandoned Super Target parking lot. We do not descend into the damp ileum of the 7th Street viaduct branded with swastikas tagged to the asses of giant spray paint swine, a caricature of Congress muzzled by a gag in the shape of the Kraft corporate logo in brilliant yellows and greens and reds, "This is not a test! This is not a test! This is not a test!" some stranger sings on the radio's emergency broadcast system. No, we do not bear her casket across the Shelby Street Walking Bridge that does not seesaw wildly as a bassinet above the Cumberland. A fleet of mechanical ravens do not rise and drop on the last thermal the city will ever know. The last river does not rage beneath us. Not a single box of emergency supplies or sleeper cars or sabotaged barges is jackstrawed or burning or evidence on the water's riddled and useless banks.

No, we do not construct a perfect circumference of bodies and hands around her grave. We do not taste her ashes, do not turn counterclockwise around that rectangular socket or flick choice tokens onto her coffin (from me: a collection of rechargeable triple As, from her sisters: a handful of glittering hand-me-downs), all of it never Tetrising neatly into the void into which her body is not lowered across which we do not sprinkle shovelfuls of soil that do not lock into place to sprout before our very eyes a new strain of invasive switch grass an entire grounds crew is neither interviewed nor drug-tested nor poorly trained to tend as my colleagues in grief and dark suits do not funnel back into their cars as rain in dramatic sheets does not begin to fall above all the black umbrellas that do not snap open like dark planets above the graves, the undertaker unoccupied with the earth displaced by her body he must trowel into the hole in the lapel above his eager and exhausted heart.

Neither do we leave her body where it lies in the street, the wind-up toys of automated vultures waddling in their perches in the gray and sullen architecture. Neither do we sing any funereal songs or turn the pages of a hymnal. Instead, we sit patiently in padded folding chairs arranged in perfect columns in her high school auditorium, hands crocused in our laps. Instead, we've had our suits and khakis dry-cleaned and pressed and we furrow our brows as we listen to the words of the chosen from a backlit podium. Her principal talks of Mary's wide smile and 4.0. Her long-haired ex-boyfriend chokes something youthful into the microphone about "how fucked up this shit really is." And when her drama teacher appears from backstage in the top-heavy Snoopy costume Mary donned for the Freshman play to perform "You're a Good Man Charlie Brown," a baby cries, the pianist strikes a sinful chord, a sneeze someone fails to stifle echoes and echoes the cavernous hall.

No, we are not constructing a nest of limbs and fine oils (we are not raising a mourning tower). No, we are not placing her body on the nest (we are not wrapping her body in silks). No, we are not pushing the nest into the center of the water (we are not hoisting her body to the tower's apex). We are not launching a flaming arrow into the sky (we won't release a flock of crudely machined crows to storm the heavens). We aren't watching the nest burst into a pyre (we're not steering the birds to her figure). We're not watching her burn (we're not watching the crows take her apart in the clicking of their mouths). We are not shielding our eyes from the rise of the sun (we don't know how to track the crows' flight through a burning cloud with our eyes). We are not propping our little girls and little boys on our shoulders for a better view of fire (we are not whispering into their ears, "Look, isn't Mary beautiful?) "Don't you wish you could fly?" (No, the crows are not responding:) *We do not!*
We do not! *We do not!*

And no, that *isn't* She who appears on stage in the midst of a bantling's sermon on free will (a vague apparition in a ray of cellophaned light, the body and bone of her atoms swimming up stage-left like a tab effervescing in a 12-ounce glass). No, that *isn't* Mary standing behind the boy performing his best off-key rendition of Jeff Buckley's "Hallelujah" above his guitar (flesh and blood, body and heart, the gasps of we mourners). No this *isn't* the moment before we see She's nothing more than a cardboard cutout of *The Birth of Venus* propped against a wall adrift in the fog of a machine no one admits to clicking on and dashing headlong and wild through the EXIT door.

Instead, we eat cheese on crackers and drink Australian Shiraz from clear plastic cups in the foyer. Instead, we make visors of our hands to shield the glare of fluorescents reflected in Mary's blown-up stills: snapshots of stairs cut into the stone of a mountain, Nepalese children beaming and bedraggled before a straw hut, a shaman naked in dreads on a wheel of stone. No, She doesn't peer at us from her portraits. The hallway fluorescents neither shudder nor blink. No one thinks to question the light. Strangers and friends wander by with their refreshments. Her sisters stand awkwardly by the door.

And no, I know nothing of the buzzard who clicks and whirls and sparks when it opens its wings. No, I know nothing of this bird some say beckons to follow it back into the quiet auditorium, chairs stacked expertly in a corner, stage lights dimmed to zero. No, I do not notice the grainy conduit of light that rises center stage; I do not descend the creaky trapdoor ladder into the belly of the K-thru-12 down flight after flight of cinderblock stairs to a passageway of earth-cut walls and damp roots. No, I am not following a Bic's fluid and flint down this passageway that does not taper like a drainpipe to a levee of stone where a nickel-plated keyhole does not flicker with song.

No, song. No, keyhole, I do not witness the dancing figures through your porthole of silver tumblers. I do not observe the swaying of breasts or the jiggling of scrotums of the silhouettes who silently toss their bodies into and around the blaze that brews in the room's center. No, cool plate of nickel-plate I press not my eye against. No, flat plane of stamped metal without key I do not peer through, those aren't her ashes the dancers toss by handful into the flame, those aren't Mary's makings that flash and flare and come alive in the air above the fire around which the dancers jiggle and wriggle and coo. Those forms do not turn white with Her ashes. No, those forms do not rub Her remains into a paste in the sweat of their chests. I've no idea what they scribe there. I won't repeat, I will not sing whatever missives that fire speaks.

And no, Mary. No, my mother. No, her father whose speech ran too long at my wedding: I do not spy the china blue urn that wobbles back and forth in a corner of the room. No, my father. No, her mother: I do not see how the urn rocks slowly to a halt. I do not see the whiskers of the mouse that first appear from that dark chamber, nor the entire body of the mouse that soon emerges, blue-gray and soft with the duff of ashes. No, Mary, you do not twitch before the dancers. No, my mother, the dancers do not stitch their hands together into a bridge of souls from mouse to eye. No, her father, your daughter does not climb onto the lead supplicant's offered palm. No, my father, it does not scamper across the bridge of bodies. No, her mother, your child does not wriggle through the keyhole and leap onto my shoulder to sniff nervously, delicately, lovingly at my ear. No, Mary, you do not cling to my button-down with your tiny, luxurious, star-shaped feet. No, my mother, the mouse does not enter my breast pocket. No, her father, your daughter does not work down from body to skinsack to bone to a thimble of ash. No, her mother, I will not dip my hands into your child's body, I will not bring my hands to my lips. No, M—, girl I loved so, I will say your name no more.

Epistle

Of course he'll deny everything:
   no snowed-under field of headstones,
No overcast gloomed by city lights,
   no yews aghast in border rows. No,
He'll say, we didn't spend the night
   huddled against a snowbank
In our down vests and boots. No,
   we never were eager to witness
That which your mythologies foretold:
   that eventually winter ends
And the dead rise, graves more
   than gateways to bone dust
And gold watches. Of course he'll deny
   the scurfs of snow that skated
Across the hard pack and how hard
   it became to disbelieve in the spirit
When the bays of ferric dogs coyote'd
   down the hills and the night watchman's
Maglite flashed to life the visages
   of the dead. He'll never admit
How I opened myself to him there
   in the hollow core of December,
Much like he'll deny it was he who said,
   "We should take our own lives
Before we grow old," that it was his
   idea to venture onto the roofs of buildings
Downtown and perch on their ledges
   like his beloved birds to retrace
Our flightpaths through the city.
   Nashville was beautiful back then:
All those windows and sky. And, yes,
   I believed life had end before I tried
To leave it. Land of bluestem grass,
   Land of the twang and tremolo

Of steel guitars, Land of churches rising
   from every corner: Look at him now,
The boy who once loved me.
   "There was nothing I could do,"
He tries to convince himself
   when he cannot find sleep. "M—,
You made your choice," he mutters
   at my ear when he finds me in his dreams,
"Thank you, my love, for saving my life."

Acknowledgments

"My deepest appreciation for the Interlandi family and all my thanks to Judy Jordan, Allison Joseph, Rodney Jones, and all my amazing friends and colleagues at the MFA Program at Southern Illinois University-Carbondale."

Grateful acknowledgment is made to the journals and anthologies where these poems first appeared:

"On the 1st Anniversary of Mary's Death," "Fast Freeze," "Forsythia in February," "the catalpas they shudder the catalpas they step from their roots," and "On the 10th Anniversary of Mary's Death," *Alligator Juniper*

"The Lost," *American Literary Review*

"Marysarias," *Apocalypse Now: Poems and Prose from the End of Days*

"Ice," *Blackbird*

"Marysarias" (third section) *Center, A Journal of the Literary Arts*

"Mare Orientale" as "Maenon," *Copper Nickel*

"Night," "Like the Dead," *diode*

"Visiting Hours, x," "Visiting Hours iii," *Harpur Palate*

"Far From the Fields Turned Crystalline By Winter," "Visiting Hours, vi" as "To Touch the Moon," *Grist*

"A Calling," *Iron Horse Literary Review*

"i shiver," "I Too Grow Tired of Winter," "when the spires of these highrises at last darken," as "Reversals," *The Literary Review*

"Visiting Hours vii," *Moonshine: An Anthology*

"Visiting Hours i," "Visiting Hours iii," "Visiting Hours ix," *Pilgrimage*

"Epistle" as "Cemetery Nights," "Salvation" as "Amen," *South Dakota Review*

"Visiting Hours, i" as "Suicide Watch," "Meditation on Balsam Mountain," *Southern Indiana Review*;

"Visiting Hours" (entire poem), *storySouth*

Notes:

"Forsythia in February" owes a debt of gratitude to Sylvia Plath's "Poppies in October"

"Visiting Hours" owes a debt of gratitude to James Kimbrell's, "The Gatehouse Heaven"

"Meditation on Balsam Mountain" also appeared in my first book, *Ghost Gear*

About the Author

PHOTO BY CHRIS WOOD

ANDREW MCFADYEN-KETCHUM is an author, freelance editor, & ghostwriter. He is author of *Ghost Gear*, Acquisitions Editor for Upper Rubber Boot Books, Founder and Editor of PoemoftheWeek.com and The Floodgate Poetry Series, and editor of *Apocalypse Now: Poems & Prose from the End of Days*. Learn more at AndrewMK.com.

www.ingramcontent.com/pod-product-compliance
Lightning Source LLC
Chambersburg PA
CBHW030530080526
44586CB00011B/384